UNCOVERING AMERICAN HISTORY™

A PRIMARY SOURCE INVESTIGATION OF THE LEWIS AND CLARK EXPEDITION

Xina M. Uhl and Tamra B. Orr

rosen publishing's rosen central

New York

Published in 2019 by The Rosen Publishing Group, Inc.
29 East 21st Street, New York, NY 10010

First Edition

Library of Congress Cataloging-in-Publication Data

Names: Uhl, Xina M., author. | Orr, Tamra, author.
Title: A primary source investigation of the Lewis and Clark Expedition / Xina M. Uhl and Tamra B. Orr.
Description: First edition. | New York : Rosen Central, 2019 | Series: Uncovering American history | Includes bibliographical references and index. | Audience: Grades 5–8.
Identifiers: LCCN 2018008331| ISBN 9781508184188 (library bound) | ISBN 9781508184171 (pbk.)
Subjects: LCSH: Lewis and Clark Expedition (1804–1806)—Juvenile literature. | West (U.S.)—Discovery and exploration—Juvenile literature.
Classification: LCC F592.7 .U35 2019 | DDC 917.804/2—dc23
LC record available at https://lccn.loc.gov/2018008331

Manufactured in the United States of America

On the cover: American artist Thomas Mickell Burnham painted *Lewis and Clark Expedition* around 1850. Today the painting is located at the Buffalo Bill Historical Center in Cody, Wyoming.

CONTENTS

INTRODUCTION

Author and historian Stephen Ambrose may have said it the best. The journey undertaken by Lewis and Clark was, "the greatest camping trip of all time." With today's automobiles and aircraft, it's possible to cross the American continent in a few hours or a few days. Not so at the turn of the nineteenth century, when Thomas Jefferson became president. The United States was only about a quarter of its present size. Its seventeen states occupied the space between the Atlantic Ocean and the Mississippi River, and two-thirds of its population lived within 50 miles (80 kilometers) of the East Coast.

France owned a huge swath of territory west of the Mississippi River called Louisiana. President Thomas Jefferson jumped at the chance to purchase it when France's leader, Napoleon, offered it to the new United States. The final cost for Louisiana's 828,000 square miles (2,145,000 square kilometers) of territory was just $15 million, or about three cents per acre. The Louisiana Purchase, as it was called, nearly doubled the size of the country when it was completed on April 30, 1803.

John Luffman created this map of North America in 1803. Due to the lack of information available, the map shows the land west of the Mississippi as only partly accurate.

Jefferson now faced a challenge. The newly acquired land had not been mapped or surveyed, and no one knew about its rivers, lakes, plants, animals, or Native Americans. Clearly, it would be necessary to send an expedition to the area to find

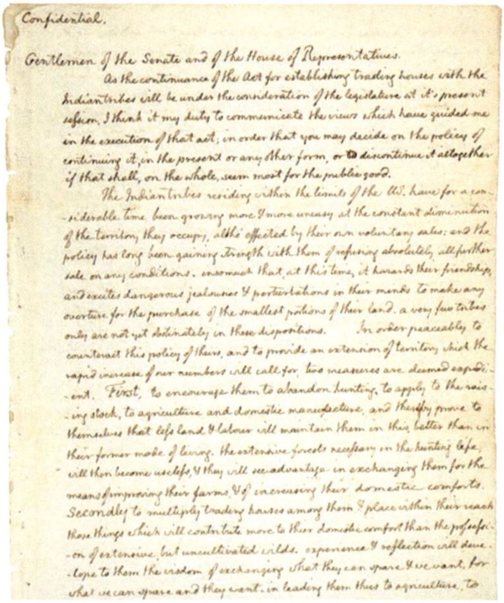
Confidential.

Gentlemen of the Senate and of the House of Representatives.

As the continuance of the Act for establishing trading houses with the Indian tribes will be under the consideration of the legislature at it's present session, I think it my duty to communicate the views which have guided me in the execution of that act; in order that you may decide on the policy of continuing it, in the present or any other form, or discontinue it altogether if that shall, on the whole, seem most for the public good.

The Indian tribes residing within the limits of the U.S. have for a considerable time been growing more & more uneasy at the constant diminution of the territory they occupy, altho' effected by their own voluntary sales: and the policy has long been gaining strength with them of refusing absolutely all further sale on any conditions. insomuch that, at this time, it hazards their friendship, and excites dangerous jealousies & perturbations in their minds to make any overture for the purchase of the smallest portions of their land. a very few tribes only are not yet obstinately in these dispositions. In order peaceably to counteract this policy of theirs, and to provide an extension of territory which the rapid increase of our numbers will call for, two measures are deemed expedient. First, to encourage them to abandon hunting, to apply to the raising stock, to agriculture and domestic manufacture, and thereby prove to themselves that less land & labour will maintain them in this better than in their former mode of living. the extensive forests necessary in the hunting life, will then become useless, & they will see advantage in exchanging them for the means of improving their farms, & of increasing their domestic comforts. Secondly to multiply trading houses among them & place within their reach those things which will contribute more to their domestic comfort than the possession of extensive, but uncultivated wilds. experience & reflection will develope to them the wisdom of exchanging what they can spare & we want, for what we can spare and they want. in leading them thus to agriculture, to

Jefferson wrote this secret message to Congress on January 18, 1803. See pages 49–50 for transcription.

answers to these questions. Jefferson wrote to Congress, proposing that an "intelligent officer with ten or twelve chosen men . . . might explore the whole line, even to the Western Ocean." This party of adventurers should "make friends and allies of the far Western Indians while at the same time diverting valuable pelts from the rugged northern routes used by another nation [Great Britain] . . . and bringing the harvest down the Missouri to the Mississippi and thence eastward by—a variety of routes."

Congress agreed, and approved the $2,500 Jefferson asked for to fund the expedition. The stage was set for the great camping trip—and important scientific journey—to come. The selection of leaders Meriwether Lewis and William Clark proved to be a good one. With care and conscientiousness, Lewis and Clark prepared for the journey over a period of many months by gathering supplies and equipment and selecting the men to accompany them. Little did they expect the high adventure, frequent danger, and incredible discovery that they would encounter on their 7,000–mile (11,265 km) trip. Their mapmaking efforts, scientific discoveries, and the connections they forged with Native Americans during the more than two years they were gone profoundly affected the future of America, giving Lewis and Clark a permanent place in the history books.

CHAPTER ONE

PREPARING FOR THE JOURNEY

President Thomas Jefferson not only planned many details of the expedition himself, but he also chose the mission's leader, his private secretary Meriwether Lewis. Lewis stood 6 feet (2 meters) tall and had a quiet, serious personality. His mother, a local herb healer, passed her knowledge on to him. As a skilled hunter and seasoned woodsman his talents would be greatly valuable to the expedition.

Charles Willson Peale painted this portrait of Meriwether Lewis in 1807. Lewis was born into a Virginia plantation family in 1774.

MERIWETHER LEWIS

Lewis was only thirty years old when the expedition

set out, but he had already handled a great deal of responsibility in his short life. By his mid-twenties, he had taken over the management of his family's farm, Locust Hill, to help his twice-widowed mother and siblings. He had joined the militia during the Whiskey Rebellion of 1794 (a rebellion of western Pennsylvania farmers angered by a tax upon whiskey that cut into their wheat profits). While still in his twenties, Lewis was also assigned to a rifle company in Fort Greenville, Ohio, where he met William Clark and served under him. By age twenty-six, he had reached the rank of captain.

Locust Hill was located near Thomas Jefferson's family home, Monticello, and the two families had known each other for years. Jefferson had watched Lewis grow up to be an intelligent, responsible, and skilled man. He asked Lewis to be his secretary as soon as he was elected president, and in the following months, Lewis was a frequent visitor to Monticello.

Like Meriwether Lewis, William Clark, shown here, was born into a Virginia plantation family, though he was born in 1770.

The president was quietly preparing Lewis for the upcoming journey by encouraging him to read the many books he had in his library, including those on botany, medicine, navigation, cartography, astronomy, and geology. In addition to these studies, Lewis was sent to Philadelphia to be tutored by a variety of experts. Physician Benjamin Rush taught him the basics of practicing medicine. Astronomer Andrew Ellicott taught him how to navigate a boat by looking at constellations. And Benjamin Smith Barton, professor of botany, taught him how to identify and scientifically describe plants.

THE EARLY YEARS: LEWIS AND CLARK

Meriwether Lewis was born into a Virginia plantation family in 1774, two years before the start of the American Revolution. Lewis would begin his military career in 1794 with the Virginia Militia and eventually rose to the rank of captain in the US Army in 1801. When family friend Thomas Jefferson first considered an expedition to explore the West in 1792, Lewis immediately volunteered but was considered too young and inexperienced to be qualified.

William Clark was born into a Virginia plantation family in 1770. Clark joined the frontier militia as a young man and became an officer in the US Army in 1792, but he resigned his commission to run the family plantation in Kentucky. Lewis, a fellow officer who served under Clark, would "rescue" him from a sedate farmer's life he did not want by inviting him to cocaptain the Corps of Discovery's adventurous expedition.

WILLIAM CLARK

In 1775, when Lewis met William Clark at Fort Greenville, Ohio, they quickly became friends. Clark was four years older than Lewis and was the ninth of ten children by John and Ann Clark. His early years were spent in Virginia and Kentucky. At age nineteen, he joined the militia as his older brothers had done. By 1795, he was a captain in the regular army. During his time as a soldier, he learned about commanding men, drawing maps, and building forts—all skills that would assist him in the future. In 1796, Clark retired from the military and returned to Kentucky to run his family farm, Mulberry Hill.

Like Meriwether Lewis, Clark was a tall man of 6 feet (2 m). His appearance was even more striking because of his brilliant red hair. Unlike his partner, however, Clark was outgoing and talkative. He loved adventure and hoped to do something more exciting with his life than simply run the family farm of 9,000 acres (3,642 hectares). His good friend Lewis was about to offer him the opportunity to do exactly that.

On June 19,1803, Lewis wrote a letter to his friend Clark to tell him of his upcoming adventure and to ask if he would be interested in serving as cocaptain. He wrote, in the often haphazard spelling and grammar of the day, "My friend ... if there is anything in this enterprise which would induce you to participate with me in it's fatiegues, it's dangers and it's honors, believe me, there is no man on earth with whom I should feel equal in sharing them as with yourself" (as quoted in Christine A. Fitzgerald's *The World's Great Explorers*).

Clark was so thrilled when he received the letter that he responded the next day, saying, "This is an undertaking fraited with many difeculties, but My friend I do assure you that no man lives whith whome I would perfur to undertake Such a Trip as yourself. My friend, I join you with hand and Heart" (as quoted in George Sullivan's *Lewis and Clark: In Their Own Words*).

GATHERING SUPPLIES

Anyone who has ever packed to go on a trip knows that it requires a lot of thought and preparation. When that trip is going to last at least two years and extend into mysterious places where the weather, temperature, and terrain are unknown and supplies must be sufficient for dozens of hardworking, hungry men, preparation is more than a chore—it is a tremendously challenging undertaking in its own right.

Lewis had already been preparing for his journey for almost two years before he asked Clark to join the expedition. In addition to gaining a rapid education in a wide variety of fields—such as botany, cartography, and medicine—Lewis also focused on the trip's practical requirements. Two days after the Louisiana Purchase was first publicly announced on July 3, 1803, Lewis left Washington, D.C., for Pittsburgh, Pennsylvania, to begin purchasing supplies and hiring men for the expedition.

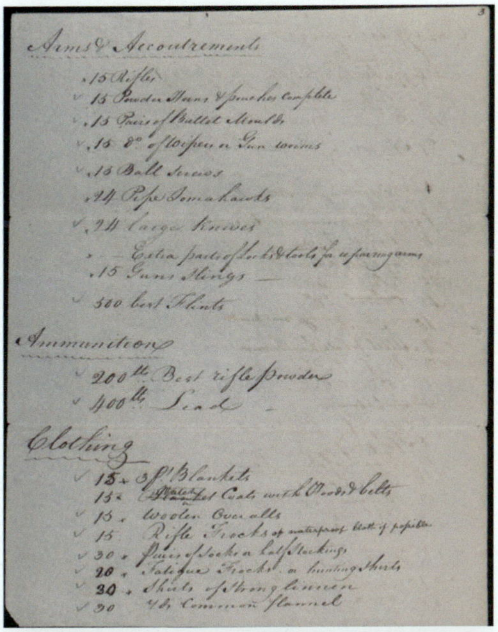
Arms & Accoutrements
15 Rifles
15 Powder Horns & pouches complete
15 Pairs of Bullet Moulds
15 do. of Wipers or Gun worms
15 Ball Screws
24 Pipe Tomahawks
24 Large Knives
Extra parts of Locks & tools for repairing arms
15 Gun Slings
500 best Flints
Ammunition
200 lb. Best rifle powder
400 lb. Lead
Clothing
15 3 pt. Blankets
15 Watch Coats with Hoods & belts
15 Woolen Overalls
15 Rifle Frocks of waterproof cloth if possible
30 Pairs of Socks or half Stockings
20 Fatigue Frocks or hunting shirts
30 Shirts of Strong linnen
30 yds. Common flannel

Meriwether Lewis wrote this supply list for the Corps of Discovery expedition. See transcript on pages 51–52.

Initially authorized to spend $2,500, he compiled list after list of what would be needed, from medical supplies and food to clothing and weapons. These lists offer great insight into the wide variety of situations expected for an expedition of this scope and duration. Scientific equipment, camping supplies, presents for the Native Americans, weapons, clothing, and food added up to almost two tons of materials that would need to be hauled along on the trip.

Lewis invested in the most up-to-date equipment of the day to help him in drawing maps and taking measurements. Compasses, quadrants (for measuring altitude), telescopes, and chronometers (for calculating longitude) were put on the list. Camp supplies came next, including 150 yards (125 square meters) of cloth for making tents and sheets, pliers, hatchets, saws, fishing hooks and lines, cooking utensils, mosquito netting, knapsacks, and 12 pounds (5 kilograms) of soap. Dr. Rush put together a medicine kit with bandages and surgical instruments for the journey. Clothing for all the men included nearly four dozen flannel shirts, coats, shoes, stockings, and pants. More than 400 pounds (181 kg) of sheet lead were bought for making bullets, along with 176 pounds (80 kg) of gunpowder packed in fifty-two lead canisters, numerous knives, and more than a dozen rifles.

Food was another vitally important supply. Other explorers had not been able to make the same trek because they had run out of food. Lewis was determined this would not happen to his group. While much of the food they ate would come from the wildlife they hunted on the trail, he also bought staples such as ground corn, 3,400 pounds (1,542 kg) of flour, three bushels of salt, fifty kegs of salt pork, six hundred barrels of grease, and 193 pounds (87.5 kg) of "portable soup" (in thirty-two canisters), which was a paste of boiled beef, eggs, and vegetables that needed only water to be complete.

Because the land Lewis and Clark would be traversing was mostly unexplored by Americans and Europeans and because they were relatively new to the formal study of science, they also needed to carry a small reference library with them. These materials included handbooks on botany, mineralogy, and astronomy; a history of the Louisiana Territory; maps of portions of the Missouri River; and tables to help determine longitude and latitude.

And, finally, Lewis purchased presents to trade with the Native Americans. A good portion of his job on this expedition was to study the different tribes and report back vital information such as their locations, languages, clothing, shelters, customs, and religions. To help smooth the way for their first encounters and build trust for future peaceful relations, Lewis bought items he hoped the Native Americans would like. These included pocket mirrors, combs, ribbons, handkerchiefs, sewing needles and thread, kettles, tobacco, knives, beads, brightly dyed cloths, and face paint. Two special gifts prepared especially for this trip were Jefferson's peace medals and certificates of greeting. The silver medals had "Peace and Friendship" engraved upon them and featured an image of the president. Lewis and Clark also handed out certificates bearing Jefferson's personal greetings to show the kindness of the "Great White Father" living in Washington, D.C.

After Clark accepted Lewis's offer to join the expedition, he traveled to Clarksville, Indiana Territory (just opposite Louisville), to begin organizing the expedition and recruiting men while Lewis went to Pittsburgh to prepare the boats and supplies needed for the long trip ahead. The approximately four dozen men eventually chosen for the trip came from a wide variety of places and backgrounds (the exact number of corps members is unknown). Some were Kentucky woodsmen, some were soldiers, and others were hunters or scouts. There were men from Virginia, Kentucky, New Hampshire, and Pennsylvania, as well as some from as far away as Canada and Germany. Most were young, single, healthy, and strong. They were separated into three squads, each reporting to a sergeant. Clark's slave, York, was also on the trip but is not listed on the official roster.

To ensure that the corps would be able to communicate with the Native Americans they met on the trip, Lewis and Clark also hired interpreters fluent in several European and Native American languages. The first was George Drouillard, a skilled hunter, who was able to converse in French, English, and American Indian sign language. Another was Private Pierre Cruzatte, a man who could speak the Omaha Indian language and American Indian sign language. Both Drouillard and Cruzatte were sons of French Canadian fathers and Native American mothers. The last addition to the crew was Seaman, a big Newfoundland dog that was brought along as a companion and to help with the hunting.

Once the boats were ready, Lewis took off down the Ohio River on August 30, 1803, heading for the Mississippi to eventually meet up with Clark and the men—the group of explorers and adventurers who would become known as the Corps of Discovery. On this initial trip to Clarksville with eleven men and the dog, Seaman, Lewis made his first entry in a journal that would provide future generations with an incredible record of this great American adventure.

After picking up Clark and the remaining members of the corps in mid-October, the group sailed on to St. Louis, reaching it in December 1803.The corps established its winter camp on the east side of the Mississippi, at River

Some of these items were brought on the Corps of Discovery expedition. The medicine kit (*top*) was similar to the one put together by Dr. Benjamin Rush, the corps' medic. Clark's compass (*middle*) helped him find longitude and latitude. Lewis's air rifle (*bottom*) was specially purchased for the expedition.

Dubois in Illinois Territory, just across from the meeting of the Missouri and Mississippi Rivers. The rest of the winter and following spring were spent making last-minute arrangements, recruiting for remaining spots in the corps, drilling corps members in army tactics and techniques, and receiving and packing supplies and equipment.

Finally, on May 14, 1804, after months of painstaking preparation and years of planning, the Corps of Discovery set off on its mission. Clark, the men, and the supplies started up the Missouri River in the keelboat and two dugout canoes called pirogues. In two days, they reached St. Charles, where Lewis would join them a few days later. Everything was ready at last. It was time for the Corps of Discovery to begin its expedition!

★ CHAPTER TWO

CONQUERING THE MISSOURI

Around 4:00 p.m. in the afternoon of May 21, 1804, the Corps of Discovery officially set off on its famous journey from the Missouri River town of St. Charles. The only witnesses to this event were a few local citizens. Forty men and tons of supplies filled the keelboat and pirogues as they rowed away.

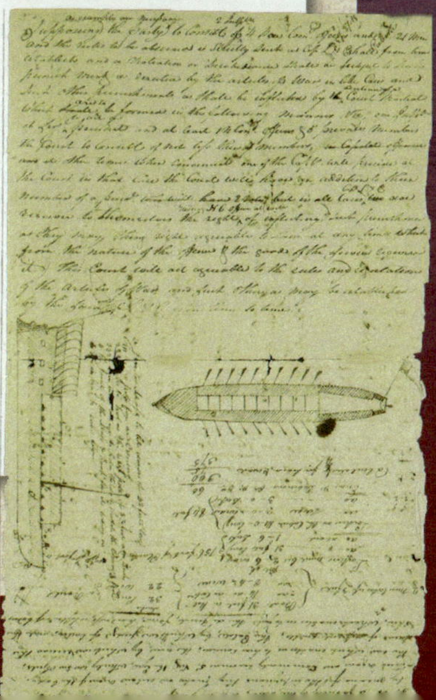

The painting (*left*) shows a keelboat on the Missouri River. The sketch (*right*), from William Clark's notebook, provides detail about the keelboat.

CHALLENGES AHEAD

From the beginning, the trip was not a smooth one. The Missouri River was not easy to navigate. Sandbars, driftwood, and sunken logs were hazards that frequently made the boats either run aground or become snagged. Some sections of the river had rushing currents, while others had still, shallow waters. The men were further tested by everything from severe thunderstorms and swarms of mosquitoes and ticks to bouts of diarrhea and cases of sunstroke. Infections were common. One man, Sergeant Charles Floyd, died near present-day Sioux City, Iowa, from appendicitis (a sometimes deadly swelling and bursting of the appendix, a narrow tube in the lower right portion of the abdomen). He became the first US soldier in the nation's history to die west of the Mississippi.

The boats averaged 10 to 15 miles (16–24 km) a day. With a strong, steady wind behind them, they could use their sails and cover more than 20 miles (32 km). A still day, on the other hand, might mean they could travel only 5 or 6 miles (8–10 km). Clark was the better river man, so he stayed on the boats to help navigate and manage the men. Lewis would often remain on land and walk along the shoreline, taking extensive notes on what he saw and collecting soil samples.

One of Lewis's main duties was to report back to Jefferson on the unusual plants and animals he encountered during the journey. Sometimes he would simply sketch what he observed in his journal, adding to the drawing informative notes and observations. Other times, he collected actual samples and wrote descriptions that he would later have shipped back to Jefferson.

A number of animals were observed on this portion of the trip that amazed and baffled the men. Many of

One of Clark's journals (*above*) was bound in elkskin. The March 1806 sketch of a sage grouse (*right*) also contains descriptions of its appearance and habits. See transcription on page 52.

Cock of the Plains.

Page of Clark's handwriting (from Clark-Voorhis note-book No. 2), with sketch of a "Cock of the Plains."

them were caught, weighed, measured, and dissected so that all the details of each newly discovered species could be faithfully reported to the president. The members of the corps were especially fascinated by prairie dogs, or what they called "barking dogs."

YORK

While no sources exist from William Clark's slave York, we do have some information about his life and contributions to the Corps of Discovery. York had been Clark's companion—and slave—since childhood. He was a large man, very athletic, and a talented dancer. He was devoted to Clark—so much so that he risked his own life to save Clark when a flash flood struck the Missouri River near Great Falls. York had his own rifle, which he used to hunt and bring in game. He must have also used it for defense against animal attacks and attacks by Native Americans. He helped with tasks that everyone else also did such as erecting the captains' tents, caring for the sails, and rowing. As a full member of the expedition he had a vote during crucial decisions.

Friendly Native Americans were fascinated by York's dark skin, as they had never seen a black man before. Indian women especially found him pleasing, a situation that York enjoyed. He often spent the night with women in their lodges—sometimes the woman's husband would even stand guard at the door of the lodge while York and his wife were inside together.

After the return to civilization in St. Louis, York resumed his previous life. Historian Jim Ronda talked about what York may have felt:

> At heart, you are always the other. You are always on the edges of respectability. On the edges of freedom. I want to say it again, York crossed the river, he crossed the mountains, he saw what freedom meant. And then re-entered a world of slavery where slavery was everywhere.

After many failed attempts, they eventually succeeded in capturing one. Along the course of the two-year journey, they also discovered coyotes, jackrabbits, buffalo, mule deer, and antelopes. In all, the Corps of Discovery recorded an amazing 178 plants, 122 animals, and forty Native American tribes that had previously been unknown to white settlers of the United States.

CAMPING OUT

At the end of an exhausting day, the men would turn the boats to shore and make camp along the riverbank. Each of the three groups that constituted the corps was assigned a job, from preparing food and hunting to setting up tents and gathering firewood. Cruzatte might entertain everyone by playing the fiddle, while others were sent out to hunt for something to supplement the usual diet of cornmeal and lard or pork and flour.

When hunting was good, the men ate as much as eight pounds of meat a day. This impressive intake was no doubt necessary to help maintain their energy for the demanding work of the long, exhausting expedition. Hunters would often return with game ranging from turkey and geese to bear and elk. Roasted beaver tail was considered a delicacy. Some of the meat was dried into a jerky-like treat and carried in the men's pockets for midday snacking.

During the course of the evening, some of the men, including Lewis and Clark, would take out journals that they were keeping. President Jefferson had insisted that the men keep detailed records. Lewis asked each one of his sergeants to keep a separate daily journal to record the important events of the expedition and noteworthy observations about the land, the people, and the animals they encountered. Ironically, the one person who had significant lapses in his diary was Lewis himself.

ENCOUNTERS WITH NATIVE AMERICANS

As the expedition proceeded upriver and the men continued to record their awed observations of the new lands, the captains began to feel a growing anxiety about what they had not yet observed—Native Americans. More than two months after the corps had sailed past La Charette, the last white settlement along the Missouri River on May 25, 1804, they still had not encountered a single Native American.

In early August, this changed. Camped at the junction of the Missouri and Platte Rivers, about 100 miles (161 km) past the southern border of present-day Iowa, the group was startled when fourteen Oto and Missouri Indians suddenly appeared in their camp. Fortunately, the visitors were friendly. Soon, an exchange of food was made and a meeting was set up for the following day.

All the men of the corps appeared at the meeting in dress uniform to impress the Native Americans. Lewis carefully explained to the Oto and Missouri how the territory no longer belonged to France or Spain but was now part of the United States. As he handed out the peace medals, he explained that President Jefferson was now the Native Americans "Great White Father."

The events of this first meeting between the corps and the natives were repeated in many future encounters with other American Indian nations. In most meetings, Lewis and Clark explained to tribal leaders that their land now belonged to the United States and that President Jefferson was their new Great White Father. Then the peace medals were handed out along with fifteen-star American flags and other gifts. Often a military parade followed, with

Artist Charles Bird King painted the portrait of these chiefs of the Omaha, Kansas, Missouri, Oto, and Pawnee Indians on a visit to Washington, D.C., in 1821.

uniformed corps members marching and firing their guns. The corps tried to impress the Native Americans with their technological gadgets, such as compasses, telescopes, and magnets. Finally, Lewis and Clark promised the tribes that a future of peace and prosperity through trade was theirs if they refrained from attacking white settlers and other tribes.

AUTUMN COMES

The signs were all around them. Leaves were changing color and dropping from the trees. The days were getting shorter. Flocks of birds were seen overhead heading south. Autumn had arrived, and that meant that winter would follow close behind. The corps was near the present-day border between South Dakota and North Dakota when they encountered the Arikara Indians. These Indians were gentle farmers who became fascinated by Clark's African American slave, York. Having never seen black skin before, they touched him with awe, wetting their fingers to see if the darkness would rub off.

The captains knew that travel during the winter would be even more difficult than it had already been. Settling in somewhere for the harsh, cold months ahead seemed to be a wise choice. Late in October, the first snowflakes were spotted. On October 24, 1804, the corps, with the Arikara chief serving as goodwill ambassador, reached the villages of the Mandan and Hidatsa tribes, large settlements north of present-day Bismarck, North Dakota, whose population exceeded those of St. Louis or Washington, D.C., at the time.

Like the Arikara, the Mandan and Hidatsa were friendly farmers who welcomed the corps to their villages. Lewis and Clark decided to stay the winter with them and built a series of cabins from cottonwood logs. They finished the temporary settlement, naming it Fort Mandan, and had moved in by Christmas Eve. The corps raised the US flag over the fort just in time for winter to begin blowing in full force. For now, the expedition was on hold until weather made it possible for them to move upriver once again.

CHAPTER THREE

WESTWARD AND ONWARD

Winter in the Midwest was brutally cold, with temperatures frequently dropping to -45°F (-43°C). For more than four long, boring months, the the Corps of Discovery was were snowed in. The men maintained military discipline with daily drills and serving on guard duty.

The Shoshone wedding ceremony depicted here is similar to the one Sacagawea and Charbonneau would have had.

SACAGAWEA ARRIVES

In November, a French Canadian fur trader who lived among the Hidatsa, Toussaint Charbonneau, paid a visit to Lewis and Clark. He hoped to join the expedition as an interpreter and bring along his pregnant young wife, Sacagawea, a Shoshone Indian who had been captured by the Hidatsa five years earlier and sold to Charbonneau. The captains hired Charbonneau for his skills as an interpreter, but they felt that Sacagawea would be most useful to the expedition. Her presence on the trip would assure many of the Native American tribes they encountered that they were a peaceful group, not a war party. In addition, the Shoshone tribe, who lived at the headwaters of the Missouri River near the Continental Divide in the Rocky Mountains, had many horses. Sacagawea could help the corps in their attempts to buy horses from the Shoshone.

On February 11, 1805, Sacagawea gave birth to a son, who was named Jean-Baptiste Charbonneau. He quickly acquired the nickname of Pomp, however. Lewis assisted in the birth and tried to speed the delivery and ease Sacagawea's pain by offering her a potion that included the powder of a crushed rattle from a rattlesnake.

LEARNING ABOUT THE LAND

During the corps' time at Fort Mandan, Lewis and Clark received valuable information from the Native Americans about the surrounding area and the terrain the corps would encounter once they departed in the spring. Through sign language and drawings, the men learned that they would be facing waterfalls and mountains soon. Throughout the winter, Clark worked on a map of the area between the upper Mississippi and Missouri Rivers and the major tributaries of the lower and middle Missouri. This map was based on his own observations and his conversations with Native Americans and traders.

Lewis and Clark called the keelboat shown here simply "the boat." The men used poles to navigate the Missouri River in May 1804.

The captains spent most of the winter months putting together information, specimens, and artifacts that could be sent back to Jefferson as soon as the river thawed. In early April 1805, Lewis and Clark loaded the keelboat, which was too clumsy to navigate the upcoming waters, with five boxes of maps, sketches, reports, soil and plant specimens, mineral samples, charts, animal skins and skeletons, horns, Native American gifts, live magpies, and even a caged prairie dog! Twelve men from the corps accompanied the boat back to St. Louis.

SACAGAWEA: BIRD WOMAN

Born around 1788 near the border between present-day Idaho and Montana, Sacagawea was captured from her homeland by the Hidatsa tribe at about age twelve.

When she was around sixteen years old, she and another woman were sold to French-Canadian fur trader Toussaint Charbonneau as wives. William Clark recorded the pronunciation of her name in his journals as: "Sah-cah' gah-we-ah." Her name means "Bird Woman" in the language of her tribe, the Shoshone.

Chabonneau and Sacagawea made up an interpreting team since she spoke Shoshone and Hidatsa and he spoke Hidatsa and French. Another expedition member, Francois Labiche, spoke French and English. So messages from Native Americans would likely have been translated into at least three languages.

Sacagawea gave birth to son Jean-Baptiste Charbonneau on February 11, 1805, while the expedition stayed at Fort Mandan. Sacagawea did more than serve as a translator. The only woman on the expedition, she proved to the Native American tribes they came across that the group was friendly, since war bands never included women, much less infants like Jean-Baptiste. She remembered trails from her childhood, and helped the corps by gathering edible plants and

medicines from the environment. When an expedition boat she had been riding in nearly capsized, she managed to save important books and papers, instruments, medicine, and other valuable items.

UNCHARTED TERRITORY

On April 7, 1805, the same day that the keelboat was sent on its way back to St. Louis, Lewis, Clark, and thirty-one remaining members of the corps (including Charbonneau, Sacagawea, and Jean-Baptiste) set off in the opposite direction in six small canoes and the two pirogues. According to PBS Online, Lewis wrote of this departure in his journal: "We were now about to penetrate a country at least two thousand miles in width, on which the foot of civilized man had never trodden ... I could but esteem this moment of my departure as among the most happy of my life."

The rowing was difficult. They were traveling against the Missouri's current, and the crew was plagued by cold winds, smoke from prairie grass fires, and hordes of mosquitoes. Often the men would be blistered by the sun from the waist up, while from the waist down they were submerged in icy cold water, as they carried or dragged the boats through shallow streams and rocky patches. By the end of April, the corps had entered present-day Montana, farther west than any known white person had ever traveled on the Missouri River.

As the journey upriver progressed, however, group spirits lifted. There was plenty of game in this area, so food was abundant, and the weather continued to improve each day. Herds of buffalo numbering several thousand were not uncommon. It is estimated that members of the corps were eating as much as ten pounds of buffalo meat a day during this portion of the journey. A serious challenge was waiting ahead for the captains, however, and it was one that could mean weeks of delay if they made the wrong choice.

THE GREAT FALLS

Up to this point, Lewis and Clark had been following the information the Hidatsa had given them about the terrain. On June 2, 1805, the corps was suddenly faced with an unexpected choice and a difficult decision. The Missouri River forked, with one stream appearing to run southwest and the other northwest. Which one was the "true" Missouri? Both forks seemed to be roughly the same size, offering no visual clue as to which one should be followed.

Traveling slightly ahead of the corps, Lewis and a few others journeyed down the south fork to see if they could find the waterfalls that the Hidatsa had told them about. If they found the waterfalls, they would know they had chosen the correct path. Two days after setting out, the advance party found the waterfalls, which Lewis considered to be the grandest sight he had ever beheld.

Although the falls were beautiful, they definitely presented a problem for the Corps of Discovery. The Great Falls, as Lewis christened them, were not a single waterfall, but a network of five falls stretching out over more than ten miles of river. Since the corps would not be able to navigate this dangerous stretch of river, Lewis and Clark needed to find a way around the falls. That meant carrying the boats and supplies 18.5 miles (30 km) of land.

On June 13, 1805, the expedition reached the Great Falls (*top*) in present-day Montana. Fast-running water (***bottom***) posed perils for the corps members, including capsizing of the canoes, which threatened supplies like maps, journals, and artifacts collected along the way.

The crew's strength and endurance were severely tested during this period of the trip. Before they could transport their supplies, cargo, and boats across the land, they first had to cut down miles of undergrowth (low plants, shrubs, and trees) that blocked or slowed their way. Wheels needed to be made for the boats, and wagons had to be built to carry the supplies. Once the corps was finally able to start moving, they were attacked by mosquitoes, menaced by rattlesnakes, blistered by heat, pricked by cacti, and pelted with apple-sized hailstones during a storm. A flash flood almost drowned Sacagawea, Charbonneau, Clark, and York. It took almost a month to get around the Great Falls and reach a stretch of the Missouri River that was safe to navigate.

By mid-July, the group was back on the river. Soon after, they entered a 3-mile (5 km)-long gorge of immense proportions. Cliffs rose on each side of the water to heights of more than 1,400 feet (427 m), and there was no shoreline to set camp. Lewis christened the place the Gates of the Rocky Mountains. Hoping to discover the fabled Northwest Passage to the Pacific Ocean on the other side of this "gate," Lewis had little idea of the might, majesty, and extent of the mountains that stretched out far beyond his immediate sight.

★ CHAPTER FOUR

CHALLENGES AND TRIUMPHS

The sight of faraway snowy mountains in June 1805 made the Corps of Discovery reluctantly admit that they would not find

Sacagawea performed an invaluable service to the expedition through her efforts interpreting native languages. Artist Charles Marion Russell depicted one such instance in his 1905 oil painting.

any Northwest Passage to usher them through to the Pacific Ocean beyond. There was no way around it. They would have to scale over the tall mountains.

A HOMECOMING

The trip from the Missouri River up over the Rockies and down to the Columbia River (which empties into the Pacific) was going to be an incredibly difficult one, and it would have to be done on land. It was almost time to abandon the boats and go back to riding horses. The problem was they did not have any horses. Their only hope of getting any rested with the Shoshone Indians, who, so far, had not been seen.

Painting by Charles Fritz - An Artist with the Corps of Discovery

Lewis expected that the Rocky Mountains would be narrow and quickly crossed. Nothing could be further from the truth.

Clark, York, Sacagawea, and a few other corps members headed off to search for some Shoshone. Sacagawea began to recognize landmarks from the childhood years she had spent in the area before she had been taken away from her people. She suspected that they were close to the country of her ancestors. On August 11, 1805, traveling ahead of the corps, Lewis and three men sighted a Shoshone scout on horseback, but he rode off before they could talk to him and declare their peaceful intentions.

Two days later, Lewis came across three Native American women. Although they initially thought he meant to hurt them, he quickly offered them gifts, and they realized he was not dangerous. He was led back to their village and was accepted with embraces and smiles. When the rest of the corps was brought to the tribe to begin negotiating for horses, a wonderful surprise awaited all assembled. The chief of the Shoshone, Cameahwait, turned out to be Sacagawea's brother. There were many tears and much rejoicing by everyone who witnessed the unexpected family reunion.

After this joyous wave of emotion subsided, however, it was time to get down to business. Convincing the Shoshone, a poor tribe, to trade horses for knives, trinkets, tobacco, mirrors, and ammunition was not easy. In the end, however, the corps was able to obtain twenty-nine horses and a mule for the trip. Cameahwait warned the men that crossing in autumn would be dangerous and the game scarce, but the men could not be persuaded to wait for spring. They needed to move on.

THE BITTERROOTS

The crossing of the Rockies would prove to be the most difficult and treacherous part of the entire journey. Guided by an elderly Shoshone they nicknamed Old Toby, the captains and their crew headed out for the Bitterroot Mountains of Idaho. In the coming days, they encountered so much misery they almost could not go on. They ran out of food and had to shoot and eat three of the horses. Each day brought an awful combination of rain, sleet, and snow. The men were cold, hungry, and wet all the time. The climbing was steep and slippery. They occasionally lost the trail. Even after two weeks of exhausting effort, mountains continued to stretch west as far as their eyes could see. The Rockies were far more extensive than they had believed, and the Pacific Ocean still seemed impossibly distant and difficult to reach.

On September 17, 1805, the corps, on the brink of starvation, met and discussed their chances of survival and

Edgar S. Paxson's *The Corps of Discovery's Camp at Travelers' Rest Creek* shows a meeting between the corps and the Nez Percé. The Native American beside George Drouillard has put his bow and shield on the ground to signify peaceful intent.

possible strategies. They were simply too tired to go back, so they kept going forward.

On September 22, the corps finally emerged from the Bitterroot Mountains near present-day Weippe, Idaho, thirteen days after they began their ascent and soon stumbled upon a Nez Percé (French for "pierced nose") Indian village. Fortunately for the weakened and dejected corps, this was a friendly and welcoming tribe. Lewis, Clark, and the rest of the crew stayed in the Nez Percé camp for a week, recovering from starvation and exhaustion and feasting on salmon. They built five new canoes from hollowed-out pine trees and left their horses with Chief Twisted Hair for safekeeping.

By the end of the first week of October, they were on the move again, this time on the Clearwater River. These waters were full of rapids, and for once, the corps was going with the current. Their progress was very swift, and food was plentiful since the entire river was full of salmon. The men lived on these fish—and became terribly tired of it, too. Happily, though, the Clearwater River led to the Snake River, which in turn emptied into the Columbia River. They were quickly drawing closer to the Pacific Ocean.

The corps, having been away from home for two years, was so eager to reach their final westward destination that they misjudged where the ocean was. On November 7, Clark wrote in his journal (as quoted in George Sullivan's *Lewis and Clark: In Their Own Words*),"Ocian in view! O! the joy! . . . Great joy in the camp we are in View of the Ocian, this great Pacific Ocean which we been So long anxious to see." Unfortunately, the men were mistaken. The large body of water before them was only Gray's Bay, a widening in the Columbia River. Their long-sought goal, however, lay only 20 miles (32 km) away.

FORT CLATSOP

By the time the Corps of Discovery reached present-day Washington state and saw the Pacific ocean, eighteen months had passed since the expedition began. Bad weather and the coming winter made the party vote on whether or not to winter in the area or head home. They elected to build a fort 2 miles (3 km) up from what is today the Lewis and Clark River. They named it Fort Clatsop, the first American military structure built west of the Rocky Mountains. The site provided nearby fresh water in a spring and shelter from the harshest weather. Since it was close to both the river and the coast they could build a salt works and keep watch for trade ships.

The expedition began to build the fort on December 9, and moved in on December 25, Christmas Day. The expedition stayed there from December 1805 to March 1806. A replica of the original fort has been constructed at Fort Clatsop National Memorial, in Washington's Lewis & Clark National and State Historical Parks. During the summer months, park rangers wearing costumes from the early 1800s lead programs for visitors. See the listing at the end of the book for the Lewis and Clark National Historical Park for more information.

THE OCEAN AT LAST

Because of stormy weather, it would take almost three weeks for the corps to finally reach the ocean. When they did, they were too tired to celebrate. They were exhausted, hungry, wet, and ready to rest. Having traveled more than 4,000 miles (6,437 km) from the mouth of the Missouri River to the Pacific Ocean, they needed to regain their strength and energy for the long return journey.

Even though their goal had been reached, the corps still had a big decision to make. Should they head back to St. Louis immediately or wait until the winter was over? Taking a vote, which included Clark's slave, York, and Sacagawea, the group decided to spend the winter on the south side of the Columbia River, near present-day Astoria, Oregon. Immediately, they began to build a log fort, which they named Fort Clatsop after the Native American tribe nearby.

Once again, it was a long and dreary winter. While there was less snow in this area of the country, there was almost constant rain. That winter Lewis reported that there were only twelve days without rain. The dampness was so extreme that clothes mildewed and food rotted quickly. Corps members passed the time by making three hundred pairs of moccasins, as well as new shirts and trousers to replace what had been destroyed by the humidity. The men could not wait for winter to end. The arrival of spring meant only one thing to them: it was time to go home!

★ CHAPTER FIVE

JOURNEY'S END

The Corps of Discovery began the long journey home on March 23, 1806. They wanted to reach St. Louis before winter set in. The trip up the Columbia River proved a difficult challenge because of the powerful currents against them and

The Lemhi Pass in the Bitterroot mountain range is shown here from the Lewis and Clark Backcountry Byway in Idaho.

the churning rapids. The hardships soon caused the corps to burn the canoes and make the trip on foot instead. They returned to the Nez Percé village they had visited the previous fall where their horses were waiting for them in early May.

LEAVE-TAKINGS

Lewis and Clark wanted to continue east immediately, but they had to wait two weeks for deep snow on the Bitterroot Mountain to melt. Finally, with three Nez Percé guides to help them, they began the long trip home. The going was tough, but on June 30, they emerged from the mountains with the knowledge that, from this point forward, the trip would only get easier.

On August 14, the corps passed through the Mandan camp where they had wintered almost two years earlier. As they passed through, they said good-bye to Sacagawea, Charbonneau, and Jean-Baptiste, who stayed behind. This was not their last contact, however. In later years, Jean-Baptiste would become an adopted member of Clark's family. Although the Charbonneaus stayed behind, the Mandan chief, Sheheke ("Coyote,"

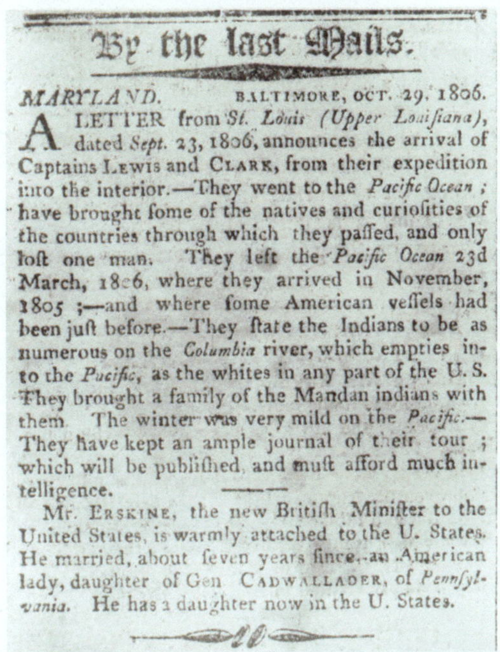

By the last Mails.

MARYLAND. BALTIMORE, OCT. 29, 1806.

A LETTER from *St. Louis (Upper Louisiana)*, dated *Sept.* 23, 1806, announces the arrival of Captains LEWIS and CLARK, from their expedition into the interior.—They went to the *Pacific Ocean*; have brought fome of the natives and curiofities of the countries through which they paffed, and only loft one man. They left the *Pacific Ocean* 23d March, 1806, where they arrived in November, 1805;—and where fome American veffels had been juft before.—They ftate the Indians to be as numerous on the *Columbia* river, which empties into the *Pacific*, as the whites in any part of the U. S. They brought a family of the Mandan indians with them. The winter was very mild on the *Pacific*.—They have kept an ample journal of their tour; which will be publifhed, and muft afford much intelligence.

Mr. ERSKINE, the new Britifh Minifter to the United States, is warmly attached to the U. States. He married, about feven years fince, an American lady, daughter of Gen CADWALLADER, of *Pennfylvania*. He has a daughter now in the U. States.

This article announces the return of Captains Lewis and Clark from their journey. See transcription on page 53.

In this painting, Meriwether Lewis wears a cape made of otter fur and weasel skins called a tippet.

also called "Big White"), and his wife Yellow Corn traveled to St. Louis with the captains.

By September, the corps had returned to the Missouri River and were covering 70 miles (113 km) a day on its swift current. On September 23, 1806, Lewis and Clark and their crew arrived in St. Louis. People there were shocked to find that the men were still alive. It had been so long since anyone had received any word of the expedition that they had feared the worse.

Although the expedition had received almost no attention when it set out, the members of the corps became national heroes upon their return. Banquets, balls, parades, and gun salutes were held in their honor. Congress awarded all the group's members double pay ($8 per month, or $224 total) and 320 acres (129 ha) of land. Lewis was paid $40 for each month he was gone (approximately $1,128 total), as well as 1,600 acres (647 ha). Clark received $30 a month ($840 total) and 1,600 acres.

AFTER THE CORPS

After the incredible journey was over and life began to settle down, Lewis and Clark found themselves going in different directions. Lewis was appointed the governor of the Territory of Upper Louisiana in 1807, but he never enjoyed the job. He seemed to fall into depression and began to drink heavily. In September 1809, on his way to Washington, D.C, to report on the state of affairs in the Louisiana Territory, Lewis apparently committed suicide in Tennessee by shooting himself in the head and chest. Some people believed he was murdered, but his closest friends, Clark and Jefferson, both believed he killed himself.

Clark, on the other hand, followed a far more prosperous path. In January 1807, he was made brigadier general of the Louisiana Militia and superintendent of Indian Affairs for the territory of Upper Louisiana. On January 5, 1808, he married Julia Hancock. They would have five children together. In 1813, Clark became governor of the Missouri Territory, a position he held until Missouri became a state in 1820. He continued to serve as superintendent of Indian Affairs and, over the years, earned the respect of many Native Americans. They often provided him with new information about western lands that allowed him to continuously update his map of the American West. Clark lived a full and happy life, dying in 1838 at the age of sixty-eight.

Most historical accounts report that Sacagawea passed away in 1812 in South Dakota. Others believe that she

lived to be more than one hundred years old and died on a reservation in Wyoming. Her son, Jean-Baptiste, was raised from the age of six by Clark and his family, eventually being adopted by them. Charbonneau lived to his early eighties. Perhaps Jean-Baptiste's parents wished to offer him an education and the chance to lead a prosperous life.

The information the Corps of Discovery returned with would change the course of history. Even though they had to report the disappointing news that there was no all-water passage linking the Atlantic and Pacific Oceans, the trip was still considered a tremendous success. Lewis and Clark's extraordinarily courageous expedition had a profound effect on the future of America's development. The expedition provided the knowledge that would make western travel and settlement a reality. It detailed the territory's natural bounty, resulting in fur trading becoming a hugely profitable business. Eastern goods found new markets as trade routes opened and the population spread westward, providing the national economy with an enormous boost. Finally,

This map of the American West was first begun by William Clark at Fort Clatsop during the winter of 1805 to 1806. It is 4 feet (1.2 meters) wide with a detailed depiction of the land and water features.

Lewis and Clark's expedition helped to establish the United States's claim to the Louisiana Territory, allowing the country to obtain even more land—such as the Oregon Territory—and further reduce the European presence and influence in North America.

The Corps of Discovery's two and a half years in the wilderness set the stage for great transformation: a

LEWIS'S DEATH

On a trip from the lower Mississippi Valley to Washington, D.C., Lewis took his own life on October 11, 1809. He was on his way to Washington to meet with lawmakers over the way he managed federal funds in the Louisiana Territory. His friends acknowledged that he had long been subject to emotional difficulties. At the time, diseases of the mind were not well understood. Some called Lewis's condition melancholy, while Thomas Jefferson described it as "hypochondriac affections." Scholars have long speculated on his cause of death. Some assert that he was deranged due to syphilis, malaria, or bipolar disorder. Others say that he was murdered.

About his death, Thomas Jefferson reflected about the great loss to "his country of one of her most valued citizens whose valour & intelligence would have been now imployed."

His grave and a memorial marker are located on Natchez Trace near the site of Grinder's Stand in Lewis County, Tennessee.

tiny, immature collection of former colonies surrounded by scheming European powers would soon turn into an enormous, influential, independent, and wealthy nation prepared to take its place on the world stage. The courage, determination, and resilience of Lewis and Clark's Corps of Discovery proved to the young country that new land awaited them, full of delightful discoveries, awe-inspiring sights, abundant adventures, untold riches, and limitless opportunities. The corps' fantastic journey first introduced Americans to the land they would come to call their own. It expanded the American imagination and sense of destiny as it enlarged the country's borders. The members of the Corps of Discovery emerged from the wilderness into a country that would soon change drastically as a result of their courageous exploration.

TIMELINE

1770 William Clark is born.
1774 Meriwether Lewis is born.
1775 The Revolutionary War begins.
1776 The Continental Congress adopts the Declaration of Independence in Philadelphia, Pennsylvania.
1783 Revolutionary War officially ends with the signing of the Paris Peace Treaty.
1800 Thomas Jefferson is elected president.
1801 Lewis becomes Jefferson's private secretary.
1802 Lewis is asked to command the expedition to explore the West.
1803 The Louisiana Purchase is made. Lewis asks Clark to join him on the exploratory expedition.
1804 Jefferson is reelected. The Corps of Discovery sets out from St. Louis, reaches Mandan villages, and makes a winter camp.
1805 The expedition crosses the Continental Divide and follows the Columbia River to the Pacific Ocean, then winters at Fort Clatsop.
1806 Lewis and Clark separate to recross the Continental Divide, then join at the mouth of the Yellowstone River, reaching St. Louis again in September.
1807 Lewis is appointed governor of Louisiana Territory. Clark is appointed brigadier general of the militia and superintendent of Indian Affairs for the Territory of Upper Louisiana.
1809 Lewis dies.
1813 Clark is appointed governor of Missouri Territory.
1814 The journals of Lewis and Clark are published.
1826 Jefferson dies.
1838 Clark dies.

PRESIDENT THOMAS JEFFERSON'S CONFIDENTIAL MESSAGE TO CONGRESS REGARDING INDIAN RELATIONS AND THE PROPOSED LEWIS AND CLARK EXPEDITION, JANUARY 18, 1803

TRANSCRIPTION EXCERPT

The river Missouri, and the Indians inhabiting it, are not as well known as is rendered desirable by their connexion with the Mississippi, and consequently with us. It is, however, understood, that the country on that river is inhabited by numerous tribes, who furnish great supplies of furs and peltry to the trade of another nation, carried on in a high latitude, through an infinite number of portages and lakes, shut up by ice through a long season. The commerce on that line could bear no competition with that of the Missouri, traversing a moderate climate, offering according to the best accounts, a continued navigation from its source, and possibly with a single portage, from the Western Ocean, and finding to the Atlantic a choice of channels through the Illinois or Wabash, the lakes and Hudson, through the Ohio and Susquehanna, or Potomac or James rivers, and through the Tennessee and Savannah, rivers. An intelligent officer, with ten or twelve chosen men, fit for the enterprise, and willing to undertake it, taken from our posts, where they may be spared without inconvenience, might explore the whole line, even to the Western Ocean, have conferences with the natives on the subject of commercial intercourse, get admission among them for our traders, as others are admitted, agree on convenient deposits for an interchange of articles, and return with the information acquired, in the course of two summers. Their arms and accoutrements, some instruments of observation, and light and cheap presents for the Indians, would be all the apparatus they could carry, and with an expectation of a soldier's portion of land on their return, would constitute the whole expense. Their pay would be going on, whether here or there. While other civilized nations have encountered great expense to enlarge the boundaries of knowledge by undertaking voyages of discovery, and for other literary purposes, in various parts and directions, our nation seems to owe to the same object, as well as to its own

interests, to explore this, the only line of easy communication across the continent, and so directly traversing our own part of it. The interests of commerce place the principal object within the constitutional powers and care of Congress, and that it should incidentally advance the geographical knowledge of our own continent, cannot be but an additional gratification. The nation claiming the territory, regarding this as a literary pursuit, which is in the habit of permit- ting within its dominions, would not be disposed to view it with jealousy, even if the expiring state of its interests there did not render it a matter of indifference. The appropriation of two thousand five hundred dollars, "for the purpose of extending the external commerce of the United States," while understood and considered by the Executive as giving the legislative sanction, would cover the undertaking from notice, and prevent the obstructions which interested individuals might otherwise previously prepare in its way.
TH. Jefferson Jan. 18.1803.

CONTEMPORARY ENGLISH TRANSLATION

We are not as familiar with the Indians living along the Missouri River as we should be, given that they live so close to the Mississippi [the US's current western border and economic lifeline]. We do know, however, that many tribes live along the Missouri. Using a large network of lakes and land crossings, they send a lot of furs and pelts far up north—where severe weather and icy conditions make the trading season short—to traders of another country. It's possible that we could take over this fur trade by taking advantage of the Missouri area's mild climate and the river's likely direct route to the Pacific Ocean. Goods brought out of the West along the Missouri could then be sent East to the Atlantic Ocean through any of a number of river and lake passages. A smart officer with ten or twelve trusted, handpicked soldiers who could be spared from our forts and were physically and mentally up to the challenge could explore the whole length of the Missouri River system, maybe even all the way to the Pacific. They could also meet with Indian tribes and begin discussing trade opportunities and agreements. Within two years, the expedition would return armed with new information on the western lands, the river, the Indians, and trade arrangements. The soldiers would carry only some guns, some scientific equipment, and cheap presents for the Indians. When they returned, each corps member would receive the standard plot of land offered to soldiers. These items would be the expedition's only expense. Since the corps members will be drawn from the military, we will have to pay these soldiers whether they go on the expedition or stay behind, so their salary is no extra expense. Other nations have spent a lot of money to organize voyages to explore the unknown. We owe it to our country to explore this continent and to try to find the most direct route across it. Since the discovery of a direct cross-country route would have a huge economic value, it is Congress's right to organize an expedition to explore the West. Any geographical knowledge we would gain as a result would be an added bonus. The economic motive for the expedition could be disguised so that the country that currently claims the territory [France] would not feel threatened (even though they shouldn't get angry since their ownership of the land is about to be transferred to us). If you allow only $2,500 to be spent on the expedition, for the stated purpose of developing new trade opportunities, few people will take notice of the project and there will be few objections to it.

T.H. Jefferson
Jan. 18. 1803.

MERIWETHER LEWIS'S LIST OF PROVISIONS NEEDED FOR THE CORPS OF DISCOVERY'S EXPEDITION, C. 1803
TRANSCRIPTION EXCERPT

Arms & Accoutrements
15 Rifles
15 Powder Horns & pouches complete
15 Pairs of Bullet Moulds
15 do. [dozen] Of Wipers or Gun worms
15 Ball Screws
24 Pipe Tomahawks

24 large knives
Extra parts of Locks & tools for repairing arms
15 Gun Slings
500 best Flints
Ammunition
200 lbs. [pounds] Best rifle powder 400 lbs. Lead
Clothing
15 3 pt. [point] Blankets
15 Watch Coats with Hoods & belts
15 Woolen Overalls
15 Rifle Frocks of waterproof Cloth if possible 30 Pairs of Socks or half Stockings
20 Fatigue Frocks or hinting shirts
30 Shirts of Strong linnen
30 yds. [yards] Common flannel.

WILLIAM CLARK'S DESCRIPTION OF THE "COCK OF THE PLAIN" (SAGE GROUSE) IN A JOURNAL ENTRY, C. MARCH 1806

TRANSCRIPTION EXCERPT

Grouse
The feathers about its head are pointed and stiff. Some hairs [?] about the base of the beak. Feathers short fine and stiff about the ears, and eye. This is a faint likenefs [likeness] of the Cock of the Plains or Heath Cock. The first of these fowls which we met with was on the Mifsouri [Missouri] below and in the neighborhood of the Rocky Mountains and from to the Mountain which pafs [?; pass?] the Columbia between the Great Falls and Rapids. They go in large gangues [gangs?] or singularly and hide hide remarkably close when pursued, make short flights, etc. The large Black & White Pheasant is peculiar to that of the Rocky Mountains watered by the Columbia River. At least we did not see them until we reached the waters of that river, nor since we have left those mountains. They are about the size of a well grown hen. The contour of the bird is much that of the reddish brown Pheasant common to our country.

PAGE 50: AN OCTOBER 29, 1806, COLUMBIAN CENTINEL (BOSTON, MA) NEWSPAPER ARTICLE ANNOUNCING THE RETURN OF THE CORPS OF DISCOVERY TO ST. LOUIS ON SEPTEMBER 23, 1806

TRANSCRIPTION

By the last Mails.
MARYLAND. BALTIMORE, Oct. 29, 1806.
A Letter from St. Louis (Upper Louifiana) [Upper Louisiana], dated Sept. 23, 1806, announces the arrival of Captains LEWIS and CLARK, from their expedition into the interior.—They went to the Pacific Ocean; have brought fome [some] of the natives and curiofities [curiosities] of the countries through which they paffed [passed], and only loft [lost] one man. They left the Pacific Ocean 23d March, 1806, where they arrived in November, 1805;—and where fome [some] American veffels [vessels] had been juft [just] before.—They ftate [state] the Indians to be as numerous on the Columbia river, which empties into the Pacific, as the whites in any part of the U.S. They brought a family of the Mandan indians with them. The winter was very mild on the Pacific.—They have kept an ample journal of their tour; which will be publifhed [published] and muft [must] afford much intelligence.

GLOSSARY

appendicitis Inflammation of the appendix.

astronomy The study of objects and matter outside Earth's atmosphere.

botany The study of plants.

cartography The study and art of making maps.

chronometer An extremely precise timepiece that can be used to help calculate longitude.

counteroffer An offer in response to another offer as part of a negotiating process.

diplomat Someone who conducts negotiations between nations.

encroachment A gradual advance onto another's property without permission.

expedition A journey taken for a specific purpose.

haphazard Random, disorderly.

mineralogy The study of minerals and their properties.

naturalist A student of natural history; a biologist.

New World The Western Hemisphere; usually referring to North and South America.

Old World The Eastern Hemisphere, not including Australia; usually referring to Europe.

pirogues Canoes made from hollowed-out tree trunks.

quadrant An instrument used for measuring altitude.

survey To measure the shape and position of a piece of land.

transcontinental Extending across a continent.

tributary A stream feeding a larger stream or lake.

FOR MORE INFORMATION

Canadian Museum of History
100 Laurier Street
Gatineau, Quebec K1A 0M8
Canada
(800) 555-5621
Website: http://www.historymuseum.ca
Facebook, Twitter, and Instagram: @CanMusHistory
The museum features multiple exhibits on the colonization of Canada including contributions made by early explorers.

Friends of Pompeys Pillar
Office:
1523 14th St. West, Suite 2
Billings, MT 59102
Mailing Address:
PO Box 23535
Billings, MT 59104
(406) 969-5380
Website: http://www.pompeyspillar.org
Facebook: @FriendsofPompeysPIllar
Visit this distinctive rock formation encountered by the explorers on their famous journey. See William Clark's signature engraved in stone, and enjoy a riverwalk and interpretive center.

Lewis & Clark: The Journey of the Corps of Discovery
A Film by Ken Burns
Website: http://www.pbs.org/lewisandclark
The site offers an interactive trail map, profiles of party members, interviews with experts, and other classroom resources that support the PBS film.

Lewis & Clark Foundation
PO Box 398
1101 15th Street North
Great Falls, MT 59401
(406) 791-7732
Website: http://www.lewisandclarkfoundation.org/home.php
Facebook: @lewisandclarkfoundation
Created in partnership with the US Forest Service, this non-profit organization built the Lewis and Clark National Historic Trail Interpretive Center.

Lewis & Clark National Historic Trail
National Park Service
601 Riverfront Dr.
Omaha, NE 68102
(402) 661-1804
Website: https://www.nps.gov/lecl/index.htm
Facebook: @lewisandclarknht
Twitter: @LewisClarkTrail
The trail follows the route the explorers took through present-day Idaho, Illinois, Iowa, Kansas, Missouri, Montana, Nebraska, North Dakota, Oregon, South Dakota, and Washington.

Lewis and Clark National Historical Park
92343 Fort Clatsop Road
Astoria, OR 97103
(503) 861-2471
Website: https://www.nps.gov/lewi/planyourvisit/fortclatsop.htm
Facebook: @LewisandClarkNationalHistoricalPark
Instagram: @lewisandclarknps

The visitor center includes a replica of Fort Clatsop based on the fort built by the explorers, an exhibit hall and interpretive, ranger-led, costumed programs.

The Lewis & Clark Trail
Website: http://www.lewisandclarktrail.com
Facebook: @relivetheadventure
Twitter: @historictrails
Find Lewis and Clark themed events, itineraries to follow their journey, read the explorers' diaries, and more at this resource-packed site.

North Dakota Lewis & Clark Interpretive Center
PO Box 708
Washburn, ND 58577-0708
(701) 462-8535
lcic@nd.gov
Website: http://www.fortmandan.com
Located at the intersection of US Hwy 83 and ND Hwy 200A in Washburn, North Dakota, it sports an interpretive center and reconstruction of Fort Mandan.

Revelstoke Museum & Archives
315 First Street West
PO Box 1908
Revelstoke, BC V0E 2S0
Canada
(250) 837-3067
info@revelstokemuseum.ca
Website: http://www.revelstokemuseum.ca
Two floors of exhibits, a heritage garden, and more are featured in the museum. Also included is visual and written material on early explorers.

FOR FURTHER READING

Ciovacco, Justine. *Discovering Native North American Cultures*. New York, NY: Britannica Educational Publishing, 2015.

Edwards, Judith. *The Journey of Lewis and Clark in United States History*. New York, NY: Enslow, 2014.

Frazier, Neta Lohnes. *Path to the Pacific: the Story of Sacagawea.* Minneapolis, MN: Voyageur Press, 2016.

Gibson, Karen Bush. *Oregon Trail: The Journey Across the Country from Lewis and Clark to the Transcontinental Railroad*. White River Junction, VT: Nomad Press, 2017.

Linde, Barbara M. *Native Americans in Early North America*. New York, NY: Lucent Press, 2017.

North America. Broomall, PA: Mason Crest, 2016.

Pletcher, Kenneth, Ed. *Nineteenth-Century Explorers: From Lewis and Clark to David Livingstone*. New York, NY: Britannica Educational Publishing, 2014.

Shea, Therese M. *The Louisiana Purchase and the Lewis and Clark Expedition.* New York, NY: Britannica Educational Publishing, 2018.

Stille, Darlene R. *The Journals of Lewis and Clark.* North Mankato, MN: Heinemann-Raintree, 2013.

Swanson, Jennifer. *Lewis and Clark: Famed Explorers of the American Frontier*. New York, NY: Rosen Publishing, 2017.

BIBLIOGRAPHY

Ambrose, Stephen. *Lewis and Clark: Voyage of Discovery.* Washington, DC: National Geographic Society, 1998.

Blumberg, Rhonda. *The Incredible Journey of Lewis and Clark.* New York, NY: Lothrop, Lee, and Shepard Books, 1987.

Cannon-Miller, Kelly. "Fort Clatsop." The Oregon Encyclopedia. Retrieved on March 26, 2018. https://oregonencyclopedia.org/articles/fort_clatsop_/#.WrlQ2GinHrc.

Cavan, Seamus. *Lewis and Clark and the Route to the Pacific*. Broomall, PA: Chelsea House Publishers, 1991.

Duncan, Dayton, and Ken Burns. *Lewis and Clark: The Journey of the Corps of Discovery*. New York, NY: Alfred Knopf, 1997.

Faber, Harold. *Lewis and Clark: From Ocean to Ocean.* Tarrytown, NY: Benchmark Books, 2002.

Jackson, Donald, ed. *Letters of the Lewis and Clark Expedition with Related Documents*. 2nd ed. Urbana, IL: University of Illinois Press, 1978.

Krist, John. Voyage *of Rediscovery: Exploring the New West in the Footsteps of Lewis & Clark*. Bloomington, IN: iUniverse, 2004.

Lang, William L. "Meriwether Lewis (1774-1809)." The Oregon Encyclopedia. Retrieved on March 26, 2018. https://oregonencyclopedia.org/articles/lewis_meriwether/#.WrlXnGinHrc.

"Lewis & Clark: The Journey of the Corps of Discovery." PBS. Retrieved March 20, 2018. http://www.pbs.org/lewisandclark/.

"Sacagawea." PBS. Retrieved on March 26, 2018. http://www.pbs.org/lewisandclark/inside/saca.html.

Streissguth, Tom. *Lewis and Clark: Explorers of the Northwest*. Springfield, NJ: Enslow Publishers, 1998.

Sullivan, George. *Lewis and Clark: In Their Own Words*. New York, NY: Scholastic, 1999.

Thorp, Daniel. *American Journey: Lewis and Clark*. New York, NY: Metro Books, 1998.

"What Was Life Like for York, Clark's Black Slave, During the Expedition?" PBS. Retrieved March 26, 2018. http://www.pbs.org/lewisandclark/living/idx_5.html.

"York." National Park Service. Retrieved on April 10, 2018. https://www.nps.gov/lecl/learn/historyculture/york.htm

INDEX

V

W

Y

ABOUT THE AUTHORS

Xina M. Uhl discovered her love of history while still in grade school. She went on to obtain a master of arts in history from California State University, Northridge. After teaching college-level American history, she moved into educational writing. She has authored numerous nonfiction books for young people. When she is not writing or reading, she enjoys travel, photography, and hiking with her dogs. Her blog features book reviews, her travel adventures, and her latest fiction projects.

Tamra Orr is a full-time writer living in Portland, Oregon. She is the homeschooling mother of four and has written several nonfiction books for children and families. She loves to read, gaze at the mountains, and marvel that Lewis and Clark trekked right through the area she lives in now.

PHOTO CREDITS

Cover David David Gallery/SuperStock/Getty Images; cover, p. 1 (flag) Piotr Krzeslak/Shutterstock.com; cover, p. 1 (scroll) Aleksandrs Bondars /Shutterstock.com; p. 3 Lone Wolf Photography/Shutterstock.com; pp. 4–5 (background) Enigmangels/Shutterstock.com; pp. 5 (inset), 44–45 Library of Congress Geography and Map Division; pp. 6, 11 National Archives and Records Administration; pp. 7, 17, 25, 33, 41 (background) Joseph Sohm /Shutterstock.com; pp. 7 (inset), 8 Independence National Historical Park; p. 15 (top) Courtesy, Mütter Museum, College of Physicians of Philadelphia; p. 15 (center) National Museum of American History, Smithsonian Institution Behring Center; p. 15 (bottom) © VMI Museum, Lexington, Virginia; p. 17 (inset, left) Lewis and Clark, 1804 by L. Edward Fisher, Missouri Bankers Association; p. 17 (lower right) Yale Collection of Western Americana, Beinecke Rare Book and Manuscript Library; p. 19 © North Wind Pictures Archive; p. 23 Smithsonian American Art Museum, Washington, DC/Art Resource, NY; p. 25 (inset) Paul Fearn/Alamy Stock Photo; p. 27 Ed Vebell/Archive Photos/Getty Images; p. 31 (top) Reproduced by permission of The Huntington Library, San Marino, California; p. 31 (bottom) Library of Congress Prints and Photographs Division; p. 33 Private Collection/Peter Newark American Pictures/Bridgeman Images; p. 36 The Corps of Discovery's Camp at Travelers' Rest Creek, E.S. Paxson, oil on linen, 1913, 68 x122 ". Courtesy of Missoula Art Museum; p. 40 (bottom) Witold Skrypczak/Lonely Planet Images/Getty Images; p. 41 Courtesy, American Antiquarian Society; p. 42 Collection of the New-York Historical Society.

Design: Michael Moy; Layout: Nicole Russo-Duca; Photo Researcher: Cindy Reiman and Nicole DiMella